VOICES FROM THE OTHER SIDE OF DEATH

ARIEL DORFMAN

Arte Público Press
Houston, Texas

Voices from the Other Side of Death is made possible through a grant from the National Endowment for the Arts. We are thankful for its support.

Recovering the past, creating the future

Arte Público Press
University of Houston
4902 Gulf Fwy, Bldg 19, Rm 100
Houston, Texas 77204-2004

Cover design by Mora Des¡gn
Cover art from the collection of the Hamamatsu Municipal Museum of Art
Cover art by Hiroshi Nakamura, "Omens of a Place," 1961

Cataloging-in-Publication (CIP) Data is available.

These poems are for Angélica, who speaks to me day after day from life, and for my mother and father who, from beyond death, speak to me in a different way. With thanks to them for incessantly giving me birth and the consolation of poetry.

Table of Contents

Two: Dust in Love

Three: A Grain of Wheat in the Silence

Prologue

Remembering How I Stood in Front of the Statue of Notre Dame De La Consolation at the Église St Germain-des-Prés

Did you change his diapers, My Lady?

From where did you get the cloth, the tender scraps of your own skirt, did you tear up your husband's cloak so the boy would not cry from the rash?

Did you go to the stream at dawn for water to wash him well?

Did you wince when his first tooth emerged from the succulent darkness of his mouth?

Did you teach him about fire and when to avoid it and when to use it well? And nails? Did you tell him to avoid nails lying around in your husband's carpentry shop, nails that could hurt his fingers, nails that could be hammered into the palm of a hand?

Did you know nothing could shield him? The other boys, the other lads, in the street and at the school, did you know that once he was out of your sight, the world would be cruel with him as it was cruel to so many of the unprotected? Did you know that time and rashes cannot be stopped, that fire and nails cannot be stopped, that there would be no scraps of cloth at the end, when the blood finally flowed, no water from the stream, no surcease or medicine that stems the tide?

I do not believe in God, My Lady.

And yet, who can I turn to, where am I to seek comfort in this age where birth is ever more difficult for us all, hurtling towards the apocalypse that the child had come to avoid, where women like you die in the streets, under the bombs, inside the ignorance, and the boys and girls are left behind to face the fire and the hammer and the hand, and pestilence rages like a prediction of walls and what is to come for us all.

I do not believe in God, My Lady.

But my mother is dead, and she cannot protect me.

She did what you did for him, for your child, and it was useless, there is only the darkness ahead and below.

And all I can do, these centuries later, is to pray that the light I have invented, the words with which we have all been blessed, will sweeten the death that fast approaches for me and all the mothers of the world.

ONE

SOME SORT OF MEETING

"diciéndose que al fin y al cabo algún encuentro había, aunque no pudiera durar más que este instante terriblemente dulce. . . ."

(telling himself that when all was said and done some sort of meeting was possible, even if it could not last more than this terribly sweet moment. . . .)

Julio Cortázar, *Hopscotch*

Pablo Picasso Has Words for Colin Powell
from the Other Side of Death

Yes, even here, here more than anywhere else,
we know and watch what is going on
what you are doing with the world
we left behind

What else can we do with our time?

Yes, there you were, Mr. Secretary,
I think that is how they call you
there you were
standing in front of my Guernica
a replica it is true
but still, my vision of what was done
that day to the men to the women
and to the children to that one child
in Guernica that day in 1937
from the sky

Not really standing in front of it.
It had been covered, our Guernica,
covered so you could speak.
There in the United Nations building.
So you could speak about Iraq.

Undisturbed by Guernica.

Why should it disturb perturb you?
Why did you not ask that the cover
                    be removed
                              the picture
                    be revealed?

Why did you not point to the shrieking
the horse dying over and over again
the woman with the child forever dead
the child that I nurse here in this darkness
the child who watches with me
as you speak
                    and you speak.
Why did you not say
This is why we must be rid of the dictator.
Why did you not say
This is what Iraq has already done and undone.
Why did you not say
This is what we are trying to save the world from.
Why did you not use
Guernica to make your case?

Were you afraid that the mother
would leap from her image and say
no he is the one
they are the ones who will bomb
                    from afar
they are the ones who will kill
                    the child
no no no
he is the one they them
from the distance the bombs
keeping us always out of sight
inside death and out of sight

Were you afraid that the horse
would show the world the near future
three thousand cruise missiles in the first hour
spinning into Baghdad
ten thousand Guernicas

spinning into Baghdad
                              from the sky

Were you afraid of my art
                              what I am still saying
more than sixty-five years later
the story is still being told
the vision still dangerous
the light bulb still hanging
                    like an eye from the dead
my eye that looks at you from the dead

beware

beware the eye of the child
in the dark

you will join us
the child and I
the horse and the mother
here on the other side

you will join us soon
you will journey here
                    as we all do

              is that why you were
              so afraid of me?

join us
and spend the rest of eternity
watching
watching
watching

4

next to us
next to the remote dead
not only of Iraq
not only of

is that why you were
so afraid of that eye?

watching
your own eyes sewn open wide looking
at the world you left behind

there is nothing else to do
with our time

sentenced to watch
and watch
by our side

until there will be no Guernicas left
until the living understand

and then, Mr. Secretary,
and then

a world with no Guernicas

and then
yes then
you and I
yes then
we can rest

you and I and the covered child.

Christopher Columbus Has Words from the Other Side of Death for Captain John Whyte, Who Rebaptized Saddam International Airport as His Troops Rolled into It

I know something about names, Captain.

Those who conquer must always have a name ready.
Even before the sword, before the gun.

I saw the island and called it San Salvador.
San Salvador because we had been saved.

I did not ask the natives—
they were friendly, they were almost naked, they were brown
under the tropical sun—
I did not ask them what they called that place themselves
I did not ask them what they called their home

And I did not tell them that they would all die
I did not tell them that nobody would ever know
what they spoke
how they spoke
the words would be swallowed
        like boats are swallowed in the tempest
        of a sad sea
like bodies are swallowed in a mine

Now they teach me their words and their songs
here in the dark of forever
I study what they called the moon and love and good-bye
I listen to their Carib whispers
and I purse my lips and I whistle and I soften the air

with the language no one has spoken on that island
for over five hundred years.

This is my penance.

And then Quechua and then Maya and then Tzotzil
and then the thousand and ten tongues that were once alive
in the lands that would not be called my name
that would be called by someone else's name
Amerigo America
and then the learning will go on
Navajo and Guaraní and Nahuatl
and the sounds that once filled the ears
of lovely maidens
to bring forth the crops
and no one today even knows their names
learning learning
until they have taught me to pronounce each last word
how do you say friend
how do you say death
how do you say forever

how do you say penance

they will teach me how they say penance
in their thousand and ten tongues

your penance, Captain?
what awaits you?

You said you came to bring freedom
Freedom. When another can decide for himself.

You said you came to bring democracy.
Democracy. When another can control for herself.

You said you came with liberation.
Liberation. When the people who made the world
            name that world and themselves.

Freedom. Democracy. Liberation.
Words.
Your words, the words of your leaders.

And then you called the airport by another name.
It is ours. We took it. We're here.
We killed the men who called it by that other name.
We can call it now what we will.
Under a sky full of bombs, another name.
Baghdad now. Not Saddam.

Saddam Airport.
Not a name I like, we like, here on the other side.
A name cursed in the cellars
where the fingers are crushed
where the head is split
where the teeth are pulled

rooted out

the roots of that name Saddam
the striker of the blow
the one who resists
the one who gives grief
the one who prohibits

all all all crying out inside that name

but not for you, Captain,
to change
not for you to decide

your penance?

they wait for you, John Whyte,
here in the glorious dust of words
they once scrolled on paper parchment stone
here in the dark light of death

they wait for you
the poets of Iraq

Abu Nawas and Sa'di
Mutanabbi and Buhturi
waiting like the rugs they used to sit on
waiting like the founts they used to drink from

all the words you did not think to use
Captain John Whyte
all the names you did not know
not even your own
white barakah
barakah related to barak blessing

you will have to learn
pronounce as I have had to pronounce
word for word

the Arabic you did not care to know
like the Nahuatl I never knew
like the Cherokee I never knew

you will have to learn

starting with the hundred words
that pour forth from Allah

Rahman The Compassionate
Rahim The Merciful

Rahman International Airport
Rahim International Airport

can you hear them
even now as you advance towards Baghdad
can you hear their voices?

Rahman The Compassionate
Rahim the Merciful

Rahman Rahim
and Salam

Salam
Peace

one of the attributes of God

your penance
John Whyte John Barakah
did you never think

they will treat you with mercy
on the other side

that the people of Iraq
might want to call their land
with the names of Salam
the many names of peace?

your penance
oh, white one

it will take you and your leaders
forever
and forever
and forever
it will take you forever

to learn the word for peace

Hammurabi, the Exalted Prince Who Made Great the Name of Babylon, Has Words from the Other Side of Death for Donald Rumsfeld

I bite my tongue and try not to curse you
I bite my tongue and try not to wish upon you
    what you visited on me and mine

my voice that ordered laws
to be engraved for all to see and hear
orphans and widows

        no no do not place that curse upon him they say to me
        they say to Hammurabi the protecting King
        those who accompany me in the green dark of death
        that is not what we do inside the green dark of death

my code
even slaves had rights
even women cast out by their husbands
adopted sons prostitutes patients
even the oxen in the fields
builders barbers sailors
they all had rights
even the oxen in the fields

my words that have survived four thousand years
invasions depredations despoilment plunder
Persians Mongols Ottomans Arabs British
the first written words

                              of history
for all to know and see

Hammurabi shield of the land
that now lies
                    broken shattered made dust
the many words of Mesopotamia

You could have stopped this
Rumsfeld Lord of the Looters
Lord of the Black Dawn

the statuettes of birds and goddesses
crushed by hammers sliced by knives
the scrolls painted by these hands
that surround me in the mother dark
gone all gone

only my words written in stone
still with me here on this other side

                    not for cursing they say to me
                    not what we do here they say

                    in the life after the dark of life
                    we teach they say to me
                    we wait they say to me
                    clothed in green gentleness
                    the mothering dark

and yet and yet
Rumsfeld Rumsfeld
who did not defend the words and the widow
if I do not curse you, who will?

the tyrant who has fled or is dying dead?
the tyrant who broke my code?
the people of my earth who cannot speak
for fear of the new occupant of the throne?
the far people at your homeland
muzzled by ignorance and dread
who pray to you, their protector?

I am Hammurabi
shepherd of the oppressed and the slaves
I am the good shadow spread over the city

Who else is there left to speak?
If anyone steal the property of a temple, he shall be put to death

If anyone steal the minor son of another, he shall be put to death

If anyone break a hole into a house, he shall be put to death

> No no no they say to me
> we do not believe in death
> not an eye for an eye they say

If a fire breaks out in a house and he who comes to put it out
cast his eye upon the property of the owner of the house, he
shall be thrown into that self-same fire

He shall be thrown into that self-same fire

> No no no they beg of me
> not a tooth for a tooth they say

He shall read my inscriptions and stand before me

                                 not a tooth for a tooth they say

may the years of your rule be in groaning
years of scarcity years of famine
darkness without light
the removal of your name and memory from the land

                                 not his children they say to me
                                 do not say it they say to me

may Nin-tu the sublime mistress of the lands
                the fruitful mother
deny you a son
give you no successor among men
the pouring out of your life
like water into the mouth of the desert

nothing lower than you
day turned into night

If not Hammurabi then who will speak?
Hammurabi the provider of food and drink
who clothed the gravestones of Malkat with green

If I do not

may the damnation of Shamash overtake you
deprived of water among the living
and spirit below in the earth
day turned into night
thrown into that self-same fire
that fell upon the children and the books

If I do not curse the transgressor

I bite my tongue and try not to say these words
I bite my tongue and try not to say the words
that have lived for four thousand years
and are now smashed in the rubble
of the land that was once Babylon

If I do not curse you

my code and your code broken in the ruins
your glory and my glory gone gone all gone

If I do not curse you, who will dare?

William Blake Has Words from the Other Side of Death for Laura Bush, Lover of Literature

In memoriam, Francesco Petrarca

I wonder about you Laura Laura
here on the burning shores of death
wonder and worry like all poets here
in these times of war

most of all my dead Petrarca
with his own Laura to lament
her gentle smile *umile e piano*

she also loved poems
like Laura this Laura

my friend Francesco begged me
to contact this Laura Laura
use the English in which I used to write before
use the English in which her throat now speaks

ask her ask her

how she can share that dance in her throat
with the man she has wed

his lips on her chartered lips
his hands on her burning hands

Laura Laura
did you lose your chance?

did the warrior husband not hear not heed
                    the words the words
                    you had once read
the graceful lake of our words upon words
shall I compare thee to a summer's day
how can poetry lilt and lull and let fly
I have given you my heart
my mother groaned my father wept
into the dangerous world I leapt
how can poetry
and promises to keep
how can poetry forget

                    when the warrior makes the mother groan
                              makes the father weep
tyger tyger burning bright in the euphrates of the night
tygris and euphrates burning bright
and miles to go before I sleep
and miles of fire before I sleep

did you remind your husband of the ravaged summer day
                              and the bride the bride
without her spring
or wedding clasp

did you Laura Laura say yes
receive the would-be warrior
                    in your bed
open not only your lips
did you say yes my love
did you compare him to a summer's day
did you gather rosebuds while you may
oh let me have thee whole—all—all—be mine
s'io credese per morte essere scarco

18

how could you not curse
the thousand ships
the death of the river and the bride
the launching of the marriage hearse
the burning daughter in the forests
in the sandforests of the night

the fire fire burning bright on the street skin of

did you despair of the power of our verse?
did he who made the Lamb make thee?
did he who made the Lion make me?

what did you murmur to him
what well of language dip and use
the night before he sent the fire
                                    and the sword
that would-be warrior
who slaughters the summer words
for which our sonnets pray

ah yes ah yes

Laura Laura

you will tell us when you arrive
            here on the other side of death
you will tell us you had not world enough
                                    and time
had not words enough
                            and time and time

and yet and yet
our hidden whispers of love
like a fiend hid in a cloud
should have been

                    eternity enough

oh Laura Laura

are yours the face the mouth the lips that could have stopped
           the launching of a thousand ships?

Salvador Allende Has Words for Barack Obama
from the Other Side of Death

I have held off these whispers, Barack Obama, till now,
I have bitten my tongue in this dusk and averted my gaze
if words like tongue and gaze and bitten biting bite
have any meaning under this grim face of the night.
Now it is time that you know what awaits you here
once you join us in the vast kingdom of the gone,
what your retreat and regret will be if you do not learn
the lessons I learned from the bitterness of defeat,
the omen I am sending your way as you fail to lead
and flail and neglect the reason you became our hope.

I had held off this warning, young Barack, up till now.
Who was I, after all, to send you words of advice?
Surrounded as I am in this dark by the many who tried and failed,
who gave their lives to change the world so the men unheeded
in the shadow of strife, the child who cries at the dawn of life,
the women and the old and the working poor, all could rise,
I am surrounded in this sorrow by those who did not prevail.
Who am I, after all, to send anyone a word of advice?

I died that day in September at La Moneda in Santiago.
The bombs were falling, and the fires turned and burnt
and I was worried about the child inside the womb of Beatriz,
my dearest daughter, I ordered her from the Presidential Palace
and only then started to rehearse in my head *en medio del fuego*
the last words I would ever pronounce, my good-bye
to the people of Chile, *mi adiós*, and my greetings to a world
that would have to continue without me, without one more word
from the man who was convinced he could bring justice and peace

to his people without bullets and blood, without widows and their
sighs.

No more words from this dead mouth, except for these few I now send
and that may not arrive in time, Barack, so many words die in the end
before they can be heard.
Back then, in 1973, in September,
as the bombs fell and flamed, as the moment came near,
when the soldiers mounted the stairs and I cocked the gun,
pay with my death so others might remain and remember,
I'd die so others might walk and ascend the Alamedas *libres*
and build with no fear at all the joyful world of tomorrow,
there were no thoughts of fire or hate for the United States,
why think of Richard Nixon, who tried to destroy my land,
or Gerald Ford, who followed through on that illegal plan,
elected by their people as freely as I had been by mine,
why waste my last breath in cursing men like them,
how to anticipate that a boy like you, then barely twelve,
would someday lead the realm that had hounded me to death,
that I'd send words like these to any American President?

The dead that keep me company say it is no use, no good.
Spartacus is nearby, Jeremiah fills my ears with prophecy,
Nat Turner rebels again and again in his dreams, brothers
whose name you would not know that nobody recalls today,
seething in the murk of the afterworld, hoping against hope
like Tupac Amaru, torn apart by four horses because he dared
to rise against the conquerors who had enslaved his people,
still roaring his defiance to the eight winds, calling out to those
who live not to betray, demanding that someone repair the world,
Manuela Sáenz, Manuel Rodríguez, John Brown, Madero, Martí,
and our Joan of Arc who knows much about perfidy and pyres,

so many more whose names anyone hardly recalls at all,
Athanios Diakos who always insists the earth will send forth grass,
all the little Joans and the small Manuels, foot soldiers of change,
they will have no rest until the living attend the call of the faraway
dead who did not betray, demanding that someone nurse the pain.

They tell me not to speak to you, the enchantment gone.
He has done it all wrong, they say, he has lost his song.
They do not bite their tongues. He's going too slow,
he's much too afraid to brawl and squall and rage and stage
a final confrontation where his foes will bite the dust.
I answer as I can, I answer as I can and must:
Not me, not I, it's not a revolution he pursues,
let him take his time, who am I to tell him to hurry
and attack and draw a bitter line in the sand?
Do you want him to end as I have, with a divided land?
And yet, I was wrong, I was wrong,
I let myself be seduced by his song.
I should have asked of him more, much more.
I gave you, young Barack, the benefit of too many a doubt,
I prayed you would not need my words from beyond the beyond,
that you would know on your own to do what I had not done,
clean up, clean out, heal a world gone mad with greed.

Before you disappear, before you can no longer hear
my words from beyond the beyond and inside the ground,
before your run ends in downfall and rout and retreat,
let this old heart beat with the earth and the stars
and the need for not one child, not one, to die for lack of love,
let me tell you one last secret found in the abyss of despair.
It is true that he who is mighty is he who makes of an enemy
a friend, mighty and wise is he who offers the foe
a way out, a door in, a bed to sleep, a meal to share.
But not without a fight. Not without a fight.

Listen to me, Barack, listen to this man who left too soon
and who never saw his new grandchild born and lost his way.

You will be destroyed. I have seen men like them before.
They will stop at nothing, they want it all and more.
Can't you see, can't you see what is being planned?
You are the victim of a silent coup, an invisible invasion
of every last corner, every last law, every last height.
They want it all, they don't care, don't you understand?
I have seen them, they will not be stopped by smiles.
You will be destroyed, take down with you all that is good,
what the little Joans and small Manuels built against the dark.
They are the same men who did me in, they want it all.
They will blow it all up, derail the train, they do not care.
They deal in fear, they do not know right from wrong.
Oh, do not let yourself be seduced by their song.

They are coming for you as they came for me.
I can hear their footsteps drawing near.
And you await their final assault ever more alone.

Listen, listen: if you are to go down, go down fighting.

You might even win.

Barack, listen to your name. Lightening, glittering of weapons,
blessed, blessing, bless yourself, go down fighting.

Barack, listen: if you are doomed, if you are about to lose,
go down fighting, so others can come after and build,
so a legend is left, a spark to start the next fire, to inspire
and bring word of a new world waiting to be born,
fight so there may be peace, fight for what you believe,
go down fighting, my friend, do not leave the dead

without consolation and the living with no faith.
Trust your name. You are not alone. Go down, if you must
go down, go down fighting, Barack Obama, my friend.

So that when you arrive on these shores
and look back as I do, you will have no regrets.

Or do you wish to face, one by one, the lovers and mothers
you did not defend? Spend the rest of eternity, one by one,
with the stories of the pain you did not assuage or mend?
One by one, one by one, they will haunt you in the dusk.

Go down, Barack Obama, go down and rise up fighting.

This time, we might even win.

Never believe it is ever too late.

James Buchanan, the 15th President of the United States, Has Words of Encouragement from the Other Side of Death for Donald J. Trump Just Before His Inauguration in January 2017

Sir: How long have I waited for your advent, prayed for someone like you to come along? All these years, since my death in 1868, I have watched each election cycle, hoping that finally my savior would appear, a man—heaven forbid it should be a woman!—who would rescue me from my status as the worst president in the annals of the United States.

Limited as your knowledge of our past may be, surely you are aware that I have been blamed for the secession of the Southern states in 1861, just as my term was ending. Unfairly faulted for the Civil War that ensued, I am now relieved to know that the presidency will soon be in the hands of someone who will, I am certain, go down in history as a leader who most bitterly divided the nation and wreaked havoc with the foundations of our democracy.

I am excited, indeed, about your chances of outshining me. If you persist in your campaign to drill, extract and pollute, if you enable the climate deniers and help to overheat our spacious skies, you will have led us, not to the brink of a conflagration that killed a mere million, but to a more substantial achievement of worldwide significance: taking the whole of humanity to the brink of extinction. That is a record that will considerably exceed my own lapses and make me seem a paragon of wisdom to future citizens (at least, those who survive).

As to the peoples' daily lives, you are likely to far surpass the harm I have wrought there as well. Many families cursed my name as they received news of their maimed or dead kin, but many more will curse yours when their well-being deteriorates as you assault the country's healthcare system.

Regarding corruption, I am also hopeful you will outstrip me. My offenses (accused of bribery, extortion and abuse of power by a congressional committee) will be deemed petty compared to those that loom for you, guaranteeing an administration rife, at all levels, with sleaze and conflicts of interest. But do not tarry over your manifest financial or ethical dilemmas. I managed to avoid impeachment and so will you, given your proven ability to convince your supporters that facts do not matter. Would that such talents had been bestowed upon me, and oh that television and social media had been invented in my day. I could have blamed Mexico for our Civil War.

Could you address two other matters? The first is abortion. It was during my presidency, in 1859, that the American Medical Association urged the criminalization of women who terminated their pregnancies, and you have the chance to revert our laws and customs to that pristine moment when the gentle sex recognized that their bodies belonged to their menfolk.

And then Cuba. I tried in vain to buy that island from Spain and then favored invading it. You can complete my dream. Extend the reach of our empire into the Caribbean and beyond, intervene vigorously in the affairs of enemy and allied nations. Pay special attention to China, where I made the mistake of being only marginally involved in the Second Opium War. I am sure you will do better when you engage the Chinese in the First Asian Trade War.

I am not alone in urging you to stubbornly follow your instincts. Other deceased presidents also entertain high expectations for your reign. Richard Nixon wishes that your slurs and insults will make people forget his own foul language, and he eagerly anticipates manifold Trumpgates that will make Watergate seem small potatoes. Warren G. Harding is certain that your outrages will go far beyond the Teapot Dome scandal, which fraudulently favored the oil companies. And Herbert Hoover, reviled for ignoring the oncoming Great Depression, is confident you will be even more obtuse: when you precipitate a worse economic catastrophe, his actions will thus appear less disastrous. He expects you will also best him in union-busting and the massive deportation of immigrants.

Presidents who occupy the top tier of favorite leaders, including several Founding Fathers, have reproached me for appealing to what they call the worst angels of your nature. They are preparing a collective message counseling moderation and praying that you are not further deranged by the power of your high office. Franklin Roosevelt believes that informing you that he regrets the internment of Americans of Japanese origin will discourage you from a roundup of Muslim Americans. Harry Truman, haunted by the ghosts of Hiroshima, would press you to abolish nuclear weapons instead of starting a devastating arms race. Eisenhower intends to reiterate his warning against the military-industrial complex—so naïve, our Ike, unable to realize that representatives of those powers are about to be blatantly ensconced in your Cabinet. And Mr. Lincoln, whose party you have terribly transmogrified, trusts that if he were to whisper daily guidance in your ear, the Republic might, once more, be saved.

I have no doubt that you will not heed him or any other meddling altruist.

After all, I send these words of encouragement inspired by your own example. You have taught me that it is better to bolster one's image in the Presidential Celebrity Sweepstakes than to sacrifice oneself for the good of the country.

And so, farewell, until the moment you join the former presidents on the other side of death, when I will be delighted to steer you to the very bottom of the heap, where I have languished for a century and a half. What a pleasure finally to be able to look down upon someone who has done damage to the United States in ways unimaginable to me in my most desolate dreams.

With my sincere thanks for all your efforts to rescue me from the nethermost abyss and from the title worst of the worst, I am, sir, your humble servant.

James Buchanan

Dante Alighieri Has Words from the Other Side of Death for Donald J. Trump as His Presidency Ends

For some time now, I've wanted to send Donald Trump to Hell. I mean this literally, not as a figure of speech. I want him to inhabit the palpable, sensory Hell that religions have long conjured up with scenes of sulfur, damnation and screams of perpetual pain from those who once caused grievous harm to their fellow humans.

The more Trump has abused his power and position in this world, and the more he's escaped any retribution for his crimes, the more obsessed I've become with visualizing ways for him to pay in some version of the afterlife.

As I mulled over the treatment he deserved for the havoc he continues to wreak on the lives of countless others here in the United States and across the globe, I turned almost automatically to the work of Dante Alighieri, the Italian poet whose Divina Commedia *minutely recreated in a verse called* terza rima *what awaited the readers of his time once they died. Dante (1265-1321) laid out his otherworldly landscape in three volumes—*Inferno, Purgatorio *and* Paradiso*—that have rightly been considered among the towering and influential literary achievements of humanity.*

There was nothing abstract about the Hell he created. Dante pictured himself personally taking a voyage into the hereafter to meet men and women, both of his time and from the past, who were being rewarded for their virtue or eternally castigated for their offenses. Of that journey through purgatorial fires and heavenly wonders, guided by his dead childhood sweetheart Beatrice, it was the Florentine writer's descent into the saturated circles of Hell that most fascinated and enthralled readers throughout the centuries. We listen to stories of the wicked as they express their remorse and experience the excru-

30

ciatingly sophisticated torments he dreamt up as suitable reprisals for the damage they did during their earthly existence.

Witnessing the infernal realities President Trump has unleashed on America, I can't help wondering where Dante would have placed our miscreant-in-chief in his afterlife of horror. In the end, perhaps not surprisingly, I realized one obvious thing: the 45th president has such a multitude of transgressions to his name that he fits almost every category and canto that Dante invented for the sinners of his age.

As I pondered what the Italian author would have made of Trump and his certainty that he was above the laws of society and nature, I was invaded by Dante's divinatory and lyrical voice. It came to me as if in a hallucination. Listening carefully, I managed to record the words with which that visionary poet of yesteryear would describe a man who, until recently, believed himself invincible and invulnerable, how he would be judged and condemned once his life was over.

Here, then, is my version of Dante's prophecy—my way, that is, of finally consigning Donald Trump to Hell for forever and a day:

My name, sir, is Dante Alighieri. Among the innumerable dead that inhabit these shores, I have been chosen to speak to you because an expert on the afterlife was needed to describe what awaits your soul when it passes, as all souls must, into this land of shadows. I was chosen, whether as an honor or not, to imagine your fate once you wind your way towards us.

Having accepted this task, I was tempted, sir, as I watched your every act in that life before death, to make this easier for myself and simply conjure up the circles of Hell I had already described in my *terza rima*. I would then have guided you down my cascade of verses, step by step, into the depths of darkness I had designed for others.

Were you not the selfish embodiment of so many sins I dealt with in my *Commedia*? Lust and adultery, yes! Gluttony, yes; greed and avarice, oh yes; wrath and fury, certainly; violence, fraud, and usury, yes again! Divisiveness and treachery, even heresy—you who did not believe in God and yet used the Bible as a prop—yes, one more time!

Did you not practice all those iniquities, a slave to your loveless appetites? Do you not deserve to be called to account in ways I once envisioned: buffeted by vicious winds, drowning in storms of putrefaction, choking under gurgling waters of belligerence, immersed in the boiling blood that echoes rage, thirsting across a burning plain, steeped in the excrement of flattery and seduction, clawed to pieces by the night demons of corruption, or feeling that throat and tongue of yours that tore so many citizens apart now mutilated and hacked to bits? Would it not be fair that, like other perjurers and impostors, you be bloated with disease? Would it not make sense that you be trapped in ice or flames, endlessly chewed by the jaws of eternity, like those who committed treason against country and friends in my time?

And yet, in the end, I rejected all of that. After all, I was selected not to repeat myself but because I was trusted to be creative and find an appropriately new reckoning for you—something, said the authorities in charge of this place, less savage and fierce, more educational, even therapeutic. Thus have times changed since I wrote that poem of mine!

My mission, it seems, was not to insert you in rings of an already conceived Hell of terrifying revenge. So I began to seek inspiration from my fellow sufferers so many centuries later, and there, indeed, they were—your multitudes of victims, the ones who need to heal, the ones you never wanted to see or mourn, whose pain you never shared, who now want to greet you, sir, in a new way.

Perhaps you haven't noticed yet, but I have. They've been lining up since the moment they arrived. Now, they're here by my side, counting the days until your time is up and you must face them. And so, I decided that they would be given a chance to do exactly that, one by one, throughout eternity.

After all, each of them was devastated because of you: a father who died of the pandemic you did less than nothing to prevent; a little boy shot with a gun you did not ban; a worker overcome by toxic fumes whose release your administration ensured; the protesters killed by a white supremacist inflamed by your rhetoric; a black man who expired thanks to police violence you refuse to condemn; a migrant who succumbed to the desert heat on the other side of the wall that you stole taxpayer money to only partially build. And let us not forget that female Kurdish fighter slaughtered because you betrayed her people.

On and on I could go, naming the wrongfully dead, the untimely dead, the avoidable dead, now all huddled around me, otherwise unrepresented and forgotten but awaiting your arrival for their moment of truth. Each of them will have to be patient since according to my plan, every single casualty of yours will be afforded whatever time he or she desires to relive a life and recount its last moments. You will be forced, sir, to listen to their stories again and again until you finally learn how to make their sorrow your own, until their tragedies truly lodge in the entrails of your mind, as long as it takes you to truly ask for forgiveness.

Your first reaction will undoubtedly be to indulge in the fantasy that, just as you swore the pandemic would be magically dispatched, so this new predicament will miraculously melt into nothingness. When you open your eyes, however, and still find yourself here, your urge will be to call on all your old tricks, those of the ultimate con man, to avoid sinking deeper into the moral abyss I've prepared for you.

Just as you've bribed, bought and inveigled your way out of scandals and bankruptcies, so you'll believe you can bluster and wriggle your way out of this moment, too. You'll try to pretend you're just hosting one more (ir)reality TV show where this Dante fellow can be turned into another of your apprentices, competing for your largesse and approval.

And when none of that works, you'll make believe that you have indeed atoned for your terrible deeds and fall again into the lies and macho bravado that were your second skin. You'll swear that you have repented so you can escape this confinement, these rooms where you have become the prey rather than the predator. You will present yourself as a savior, boast of having singlehandedly concocted a vaccine against accountability, discovered a manly cure for the terrors of Hell. You'll dream—I know you will—of reappearing victorious and, of course, maskless on that White House balcony.

This time, though, it just won't work, not here in this transparent abode of death. And yet you will certainly try to hurry the process up because you'll know—I've already decided that much—that those you ruined while you were still alive are only the start of your journey, not the end. You will become all too aware, while you spend hours, days, years, decades with the men, women and children you consigned to an early mortality and permanent grief, that a multitude of others will be arriving, all those who will perish in the future due to your neglect and malevolence.

They will, I assure you, snake endlessly into your mind, accumulating through many tomorrows, all those who are yet to die but will do so prematurely as the brutality you worshipped and fueled takes its toll, as the earth, heavens and waters you ravaged exact heat waves of revenge—hurricanes and droughts and famines and floods, ever more victims with each minute that slithers by, including the women who will die in botched back-alley abortions because of your judicial nominations. The decades to come are already preparing to welcome the legions of your dead.

That is the despair I imagine for you, now that I am no longer the man bitterly exiled from his beloved Florence. The centuries spent in the afterlife have evidently softened me into compassion for those who have sinned. Beatrice, the love of my life, would have admired my transformation, the one that, as you are ground down and down, will also allow you to be lifted up and up until you really do repent, until you beg for an absolution, which (if you are truly sincere) will be granted.

Even so, even as I speak and divine, I find myself eaten by a worm of doubt. This, I am being told, has been tried before. The mists of time are filled with men who, like you, thought they were gods and who, upon their demise, were led howling into rooms overflowing with the lives they broke, with the irreparable damage they wrought. And these criminals—Benito Mussolini, Mao Zedong, Augusto Pinochet, Napoleon Bonaparte, Andrew Jackson, Saddam Hussein, Joseph Stalin, Idi Amin (oh, the list is endless!)—never left the twisted mirror of their own penitential rooms.

They are still stagnating in them. That's what's being whispered in my ear, that the redemptive prophecy of Dante Alighieri will never come true for you, Donald Trump. Perhaps like those other accursed malefactors, you will refuse responsibility. Perhaps you will continue to claim that you are the real victim. Perhaps you will prove as incorrigible and defective and stubbornly blind as they continue to be. Perhaps there is an evil in you and the universe that will never completely abate, a cruelty that has no end. Perhaps when pain is infinite, it is impossible to erase.

I fear, then, that it may be unkind to promise any kind of justice when there will be none for those who stand in line hoping to meet their tormentor on the other side of death. Why, I ask myself, resurrect the dead if it be only to dash their hopes again and again?

And yet, what else can I do but complete the task given to me? Of all poets, I was chosen because of the *Divina Commedia* that I wrote when I was alive and banished from Florence because I descended into the Inferno and climbed the mount of Purgatory and caught a glimpse of what the sun and stars of Paradise looked like. I was chosen from the fields of the dead to prepare these words for you as a warning or a plea or a searing indictment, an assignment I accepted and cannot now renounce.

What's left to me, then, but to conclude these words by responding to the one objection you might legitimately raise to my picture of your fate in the afterlife? I imagine you crying out—"But Dante Alighieri," you will say, "the future you've painted will take forever."

And I will answer: Yes, Donald J. Trump, it will indeed take forever, but forever is all you have, all any of us have, after all.

TWO

DUST IN LOVE

"polvo serán, mas polvo enamorado"

(dust they will be, but dust in love)

Francisco de Quevedo, *Amor constante más allá de la muerte*

Mumtaz

I am Shah Jahan, once king of the Universe, conqueror of Kandahar and builder of the gardens of Shalimar, I am and once was Shah Jahan and now I am dying, I die as I look at her, the crown that was Mumtaz, I am already dead.

To describe her is to sin.

To refuse words is an even greater one.

One word, then: alive.

She was more alive than any bird is now—and now, now as well, even as I look upon the living light of her tomb—more alive than all the birds that I have seen in seventy-six years of life than the birds that flock the air above and between and below and again above her four towers, more alive than I will ever be, ever have been, changing with each ray of sun and cover of cloud and nightfall and dawnrise, eternal in each moment, eternal and serene.

I would rather have lost my kingdom than having lost sight of my lost love.

I am Shah Jahan, son of Jahangir and father, alas, of Aurangzeb, seizer of the world, and sixth Emperor of this Mughal dynasty, I am and once was Shah Jahan, the king who lost his kingdom and has but one regret.

For twenty-two years, I watched the prophecy of mounting stones, one after the other. The first thing I saw in the morning when I rose, the last thing I saw at night when I went to sleep—

like now, like now as I lay dying in the arms of Jahanara, one daughter at least, one child who shared the womb of Mumtaz, one at least, who did not forget this old man.

Stone upon stone, what I saw every day, better to watch that mansion for the dead rising up than to risk the mother of my fourteen children visit me in my dreams. Sweet to have her again and the same smile with which she greeted me the first time—I was fifteen and she a year younger. Betrothed for five years, five years she told me, we should wait five years so she could slowly cease to be Arjumand Banu and ease into becoming my Mumtaz, five years so the next twenty would be forever years, so there would be no one but her. Sweet, so sweet and wise, the dream and her body in the dream, but more bitter to awake and find her gone. With this recurring consolation: from my bed to witness the breathing white marble of her mausoleum as it shimmered up. Every day I could spare and so many I could not, spent on her memorial and memory and memories of her. Each gem selected personally by me, a homage. Each arch of Jali approved personally by me, a vow. Each scroll of Persian script read personally by me, a promise. Surround her with gates of light, the four rivers of paradise. So she would remain with me while I remain, so she can be here now as I die, here and there as I feel darkness seep into me, so she will be waiting, saying goodbye and also waiting on the other side, when I join her, the resident of paradise.

I am Shah Jahan and I will soon walk into the Banquet Hall of Eternity.

O Noble, O Magnificent, O Majestic, O Unique, O Eternal, O Glorious, will you deny me the sight of her one more time?

I will never more wake up and see once more stone set upon stone, across the river and the plain of Agra, never again awake in this room in the Red Fort on this hill in Agra, never again examine through the frame of this window—all other rooms are forbidden to me by my son—the granite from Bukhara and turquoise from Tibet, the jasper and malachite that inlayers came to prime, the flowering lattices as white as her soul, so the poets said—though they lied as poets lie, as nothing was and is and can be as white as her soul. Slant the minarets thus, I said to Ustad Ahmad Lahauri, slant them slightly outward. So if they fall (as I must fall and die and decline, even I, Shah Jahan, once King of the Universe), so if they fail and fall, they will not fall upon her, my Mumtaz. May nothing but honey fall on her. May only milk and honey fall on her from the sky. May the stones turn all light into milk and all rain into honey. May the stars compete with the moon in their envy of her ravishment in the night. Reject the stone that is not perfect, that does not absorb and reflect and reject and subsume the bright. Refuse the slab that does not fit, make sure the soft fire of color is both rose and white, so the sun will stay with her and keep her warm even in the winter of her bones and my bones, now that I could not rub her feet when they grew cold, make sure each last carving is flawless so she will have company while she waits for me, the ninety-nine names of God to guide her while I wait.

I would rather have lost my kingdom than having lost sight of my lost love.

This is true. But she would have told me to be careful. Not to neglect the affairs of state so I could watch over the building, day by day, afternoon through night, cloud and rain, and summer beating down. That's what she would have whispered. If she had been there.

I looked at the men working day in and out, spring and fall turning, for twenty-two years I watched the stones rise seamlessly and then the gardens, I looked out onto my Mumtaz and turned my back on taxes except to demand more for her casket and tomb, I turned my back on wars, except to wage those which would bring me more translucent marble from Jaipur, more craftsmen from Balochistan and artisans from Persia, I tried not to listen to disputes and petitions and petty power. I only had eyes for the mosaic of my love. I worshipped each shining amulet of rock and every curl and curve of the calligraphy, I asked Allah, may his name be blessed, to grant me time to complete her tomb and mine, so she could be there for all those young who have yet to discover love and all the old who still hope to love beyond this life.

I did not have eyes at the back of my head.

Behind me, as I watched the laborers and masons into the night, behind me, he was talking to the generals, he was conspiring with the courtiers against his father and his brothers, behind my head he was consulting the imams, Aurangzeb, whose name I shall not bite bitterly.

He came from inside her.

I shall not deign even to damn him, the son who did what needed to be done, what his brothers would never have done and thus will not rule over one inch of the Empire, he did to me what needed to be done to a father so in love with the dead that the living were forgotten.

He does not, did not, will never understand what it means to be in love, that word love, that word alive, what rolls in his mouth like the corpse of a tongue, he understands nothing. He understands nothing, and this is his punishment.

41

You would understand nothing, Aurangzeb, even if you spent nine months inside the temple of your mother, a place more beautiful than Samarkand, more luminous than the tomb of Timor. This is all you knew: that I had no eyes at the back of my head, this he understood as he bent his knees and twisted his soul towards Mecca. So little that his prayers taught him: to insinuate, when he rose from bowing to God, at first merely to insinuate, then suggesting between clenched teeth, then more than murmuring, then finally bursting the saliva of his thoughts into a word.

Not the word, alive, that he does not understand, will never know what it means.

Sacrilege, that word. His favorite word.

For a woman, to do all this for a woman. Haram for our religion, a betrayal. Idolatry. Mortal man cannot represent the human figure. God alone, may He be blessed, only God can do this with the clay of our flesh. And my father, Aurangzeb said, first thought and then said, my father, Shah Jahan, is doing something worse than blasphemy, making of a mere human figure— a woman, a mere woman, even if she was my mother—making her into a goddess. Aurangzeb, her son and mine, gathering armies to defeat his brothers, gathering jailers to imprison his father, gathering his haunches to mount the Peacock Throne.

I did not see him.

I did not hear him.

My back was turned.

She was not there, my Mumtaz, to provide eyes.

I can say over and over that she is more alive than I am, than birds blessing the sky, but she was not there, my Mumtaz, not here by my side.

She was not here, my Mumtaz, my crown, to provide ears.

I can say she is more alive than ever, but she did not whisper in my ear, she did not say beware, beware, Jahan, beware.

She was dead.

How can I say this, dare as I die in this month of Rajab to decree this, that she is dead.

She could not receive news from the eunuchs, she was not there. She was not there to stare down into the courtyard and read his lips, see our son walking around the fountain, his head haughty as he cast his eyes down, waiting to pounce when I fell ill.

She was not here, my beloved, to tell me what to do, who to fear, who to punish, who to trust, how to stop him.

She was in the shrine I was building for her and for me. She could not be my eyes and ears, could not be my hands and feet, my skin, her skin.

I was blind and deaf without her.

My back turned on the affairs of the world until every last stone was in place, each juncture of each stone with stone, like her body and mine, each stone making love to the stone above and the stone below and the stone to the west and the stone to the south until the dome designed by Ismail Afandi went up. I con-quered provinces and levied taxes and issued edicts, oh, I pretended to rule, I planned and built the Garden of Grapes, I designed the Pearl Mosque and the red sandstone of the Great Mosque of Vazir Khan at Lahore, I met Sultan Murad the Fourth in Baghdad but only so I could steal his main Ottoman architect, I visited my summer residence in Kashmir, but all I saw in the spring near Srinagar was the water of my Mumtaz, I smelled jasmine and only smelled her, I plucked the violets and the roses and it was her, always her, urging me to hurry back and make sure nothing went wrong with what was to be her final resting place, like the resting places I built while she was alive so that travelers would not be weary, like the hospitals she had me foster so that the sick would be cared for, so that other women would not watch their blood flowing from the source and center of their life as the blood flowed from inside her as she died, do I dare to decree that it is true, that she really died?

My back was turned on the kingdom, and my eyes existed only for the memory of Mumtaz.

While Aurangzeb prepared my prison and his palace, his palace and his haunches for a long reign.

Do I have regrets?

Only that she is not with me now.

Do I repent of what I did?

I would do it all over again, every first and final lotus minute.

I say this, Shah Jahan, once Lord of the Universe, Shahanshah Al-Sultan al-'Azam wal Khagan al-Mukarram, I say this, as I lie dying in the arms of my daughter, the girl my wife gave to me so she could care for this man who is so alone and yet never alone,

44

like the sun and the stone, like the stone and the stories, the girl her mother left me so I would not be alone.

Though I will always be alone.

Until I cross the river of death and find her.

I say this, Shah Jahan, once and no longer Lord of the Universe, Shahanshah–e-Sultanat Ul Hindiya wal Mughaliya, grandson of the great Akbar and son of Jahangir, I dare to say, I who was the fifth Emperor of the Mughals, I dare to say that I am alone now that my eyes are closed and I cannot see her over there, across the river Yamuna and the plain of Agra, I dare to say that like all men on this earth I must die alone.

Ah, but behind me.

Behind me then, behind us, she and I, look, come and look, behind us what we left behind so others can understand, so young and old lovers tomorrow and beyond, we leave behind an asylum where all past sins and weary eyes are to be washed away, we leave behind so you can try and understand, we leave behind us, Mumtaz and I, come and look and try to understand, we leave in front of us and behind us the solace of the Taj Mahal.

Ashes to Ashes

He had said he would love her beyond death, but she didn't believe him.

"I knew it wasn't true," her ashes said to her or to what was left of her, or maybe she was the one who, a bit sadly and dispersed, whispered the words to the residue and sift of her life as it was carefully poured into a jar where her husband's remains—according to both their wills and wishes—had been waiting for ten years now. "But part of me," said the dust unto dust she was on her way to becoming, "wanted it to be true."

And then someone on earth, someone of flesh and blood, perhaps a relative, perhaps a friend, perhaps just an employee eager to go off and drink some coffee, someone she no longer remembered clamped the jar shut and total darkness settled in.

She didn't have time to be afraid.

From somewhere nearby, she felt (but how could she feel anything if she was dead?) she felt a hand in her hand (but her hand had been burnt to cinders and scraped past recognition), a hand in her incinerated hand and skin and the whorls of her fingerprints and the world at her fingertips, let me repeat what she felt and insist it was a hand that reached out to her from the middle of the end of the end. And then another hand began to soften towards what was once her face and no longer existed, blurred it out of nothingness and memory, let me insist that the fingers she had once known and cooked for and entwined with were breathing music into her lips and reminding her hair what it was like to be recollected in tranquility. And a leg was rubbing unmistakably against her leg and she could smell him again in the night, and he was like a wind, as was she, blowing from inside eternity, and she knew, as her shoulders and back and full breasts knew as they began to grow, she knew, as the birds of her eyes knew as they began to scatter towards the light, she knew that she was not alone, and they embraced, they embraced and she knew, she knew that he had not lied, she knew that I was telling the truth when I promised that I would love her beyond death.

Is There a Place Your Lips Go?

Is there a place your lips go
when I cease to kiss and miss you,
when you not think of me,
when you do not drink me,
is there a place into which you disappear
and yet glow?

Is there a land where colors moan
once they are hoarse and discarded,
unused, that ochre, for the Madonna's robe,
brushed over by another red or green tone
under which the Child will wither and hide?
Where do they slip, the colors between the rainbow
that the painter no longer claims as his own?

Is there a hell where the eyes of the animals
captive in a zoo flee and stray when they die?
A hideaway for the paws of bears, the jaws of sharks,
a place tinged with desolation and despair
where caged birds lose their claws as they sink
into the drowning ark where other sighs
and paws and jaws await their decease?
Forbidden to join the heaven of those
who roamed and raged free in the wild,
the howls of each animal in each last zoo,
imprisoned after death as they were in life,
is there yet another abyss awaiting their skin?

Do they bond with the souls of trees
felled before their time, martyred by the axe,

or brooding on the fire and the bomb?
Is there a land where forests go
when they are mashed to pulp and then to thin
crisp paper upon which we depict their fate?

Is there a land where poems go
when they remain unfinished, left for dead?
Is that where they meet shipwrecked stories,
abandoned by their authors, drifting
like drunken derelicts under bridges of refuse,
motherless and without a home,
as if a mother had never carried their weight,
as if they had never been blessed by birth?

Is that where you went, my love,
when I stopped holding you,
when you stopped folding me,
when we no longer flow
into each other like water and lake,
when I forsake life and you fade away,
is that what happens to those who die
without a hand in their hand and a heart nearby?

Seek me in the land of discarded colors
and I will seek you in the forest of forgotten trees.
Seek me among the stories that remain unfinished
and I will seek you in the syllable seas of broken verse,
and among the elephants lost in the final dusk.

Will we find each other then, love, my love?
Will I see your face, complete, just one more time,
before I cease to breathe and you cease to wake?

Look for me as I look for you.

Look for me in the forest of forgetfulness
And I will find you in the last color left on earth.
I swear I will set sail for that endless abyss
and find you in the last elephant left on earth.

And then and then and then again
                                    and perhaps yet again
I will write you, and you will give me birth.

Long Forgotten

He remembered her that summer in the hammock, both of them swaying gently in the breeze, though there was no breeze in his memory, and therefore, it must have been the slight swing of their bodies as he turned the page of the book they were reading. He had always been a fast reader and reached the end of the two pages before she did and waited for her to catch up, trying to guess by her eyes and the flutter of her heart the words she was absorbing, almost pursing his lips with hers as the syllables slipped into her and therefore, he hoped, into him. That motion also must have contributed to the hammock's movements, the hint of their luscious bodies rubbing against each other in anticipation of what they might do that very night in the back of his father's car if they were lucky enough to finagle it for the evening. That's what he remembered, the summer and the hammock and the book and her eyes dropping to the last line interrupted at the bottom, and he had guessed right and turned the page and continued to the top simultaneously with her, both of them in sync then as they were in love now, forty years later, that's what he remembered above all, above all he remembered her.

While at the same time knowing it could not be true.

He had not met her till the next winter. She could not have shared the hammock or the book or the pursed lips or the breeze that wasn't a breeze but their bodies, by then his dad had lost his job and the family had been forced to leave that house and the apartment where he had introduced the new girl-friend to his parents and brothers several months after they met had no trees and no hammocks, they had sold the hammock second hand, a cut-rate price to the people who came to rent the house his family had to vacate. And he had gone back a few years later to show the trees and the hammock to the woman who was now his fiancée, he had sneaked past the gate with her, and there was nothing to show: the trees had been cut down, who knows what the new tenants had done with the hammock, the place where he had spent many summers reading under the leaves and the sky blue with clouds, gone, all gone, not even birds anymore. And she had kissed him and consoled him and said it did not matter, they would be the hammock for each other, they would be the book together, they would sway and swing and swim towards the future and one day, who knows, might afford a house and two trees and a hammock and the leisure to read under clouds or just look up at the constellations and wonder if on other planets in faraway galaxies anybody could be as happy as they were. And they did, they did manage it—but not that summer, not those trees, not that hammock, not that book.

She had not been there, she could not have been there, they had not yet met.

Even so, the memory persisted.

He decided not to tell her. He did not want her to deny what he persistently remembered, to destroy his dream unwittingly, to apply her logical, practical mind to his fantasies. He did not want her to think what might possibly be true: that he was going mad.

But it wasn't that, madness, that's not what that memory of summer and hammock was about.

He realized it as soon as he decided not to confide it to her, recount the images in his head that did not, that could not, perhaps never would, correspond with reality and chronology and timelines and years and dates, with before and after. It was not that he was crazy.

It was that he was crazy about her.

That after all these decades of joy together, getting better all the time, you've got to admit it's getting better, getting better all the time—even that Beatles song, he had learned it before he had set eyes on her at that café, her hair flashing as she turned from the two desultory young men who were courting her and looking straight at him with a derisive look—the derision for the young men, not for him—as if to say, you can do better than these two dolts, let's see if you can make me laugh, if you can make me laugh then I will be yours forever. That memory of the café, she could confirm it and often did. They had been over it many times, they had told that tale meticulously to their children, how he had come up to her and said, I can't help but notice that you are missing something, and she answered, oh yes, what? And he said, laughter, you are missing a good laugh, and she had been silent for a second and then: so you're a mind reader? and he had responded, I read everything, but not minds, but I can give it a try, and then she had stood up and said, a try or a trial, and he had said, a try, a trial, a tray, a trail, a train, a troll, let me be your troll—and it had been that last repeated word, troll, that had done it, she delivered a courteous good-bye to the two boring young men and took the hand he was offering her and walked out of the café and into his life, their life. Along with that memory, however, he had juxtaposed and interposed and superimposed another one, another that could not be, had not been, possibly would never be: that she had been present when he had first sung, you have to admit it's getting better, getting better all the time, and that was impossible because that song had taken him by storm when he was fourteen, seven years before they had crossed destinies in that café, and even so he remembered her throating the song, initially as a whisper and then chorally and louder with him, they had sung it together, he could see her next to him dancing it with her head, frolicking it with her hips, coming nearer and then farther away, he could not recall ever having sung it without her lungs belting it out in unison or a little bit behind his own singing, just like when they read together. All of it true, but that had been later, much later, when they had begun to exchange the songs they loved and knew by heart and some they had adored already and some were new to each of them, but the songs were always renovated, no matter how old and tested they had been in the past, because now they were pooled and

53

redistributed and enjoyed as mutual and communal and combined. Yes, they had carved up their repertoire and devoured it, but later, later, not when he had first heard the song and then spent years singing it without her presence. So how could he remember that she had been so carnally, full-throatedly, chirpingly present when he had first heard "Sergeant Pepper's Lonely Hearts Club Band"? He had been fourteen, and she had been in another city and was twelve at that time, she could not have been in his living room or on the dance floor or at school or by the radio or the jukebox, all the places he recollected her comforting his lonely heart. Just as he remembered her singing "Dixieland" with him and his mother at the piano, long forgotten, look away, look away, when he was seven, seven years old and singing along with his mother, and he looked back, he did not look away, he looked back at that scene and there she was, the love of his life, holding his hand and echoing his times long forgotten, look away, look away, look away, Dixieland.

Crazy?

No, just crazy about her.

Crazy that she had not been there all his life, had not been there at his birth. The image came almost immediately, disavowing the sacrilegious thought of her absence: he saw her standing there, oh boy, standing by the midwife or the doctor or whoever had been there and was just a blur, they were all vague silhouettes, hardly shadows even, except for her, she had helped bring him into this world, she had heard him cry and breathe and blessed the breast and the milk and the warm hands that greeted him, she had been there, he knew it was a hallucination, he knew he was time travelling in his mind, mixing up childhood and baby talk and singing adolescence and summers and hammocks, he was creating a false past, he was making a life for himself where he could say we have been together all my life, even if she had been born two years after he had, and he could not imagine that he had been present at her birth only her presence at his, crazy, yes, he was going crazy, he was living the past as if it were the present, he refused to believe there was anything he had done apart from her, he refused a life in which she had not been there to chuckle at his jokes and coddle his body and generate three extraordinary and utterly different children, he refused to allow her to be long forgotten, refused to look away, refused a summer and a sky and two trees that she could never have shared, he could not conceive an existence without her hand in his, stretching forward into eternity but also backwards to the origins.

And yet did not dare to tell her what he was thinking.

Did not want her to refute memories that were much stronger than anything real he could check and endorse through photos and calendars and the testimony of others.

He could not help himself, could not control the images of her in every minute of his life up to the moment of that café when she had first lighted up the air around him and sent him that challenge in a glance, infinity in two eyes blazing with desire to be rid of the two boring young men and live the adventure of love with him.

He could not help himself.

But was sad that this was the one thing he could not reveal.

Preferring to nurse those images of a false past in isolation than subject them to her scrutiny, because then he would be bereft, shipwrecked, his memories punctured, unable to continue, he would have to agree that the time without her was long forgotten, he would have to look away, look away, look away.

"What are you thinking, love?" she asked.

"Nothing."

"You know what I was thinking, little troll?" she said.

"When this little troll of yours told you that he could read everything but minds, I meant it. So I won't even try to guess."

"I was thinking, my dear, my darling, my little troll who cannot read minds but everything else, I was thinking about that summer when we were in the hammock in your parents' house, and there was no breeze, but the hammock would sway with our bodies. Ever so slightly, love, because it was really just that I was reading slower than you and you would move with me as I caught up before turning the page. And those two trees and the leaves above, and you said, the leaves in the trees are singing under the sky, you said, men call them leaves because they don't know the word, they don't know the word for bird yet. What a lovely summer that was. Do you remember that summer we spent together, when we were young, you and I?"

"Yes," he said. "Yes, I remember."

Glitch

So this is how it happened
This is how the Universe was formed

Starting so simply

like writing an email to a son
                                        faraway

Like writing an e-mail to my son
in North Carolina
from
            San Pedro de Atacama
this oasis in the middle of the driest
                                        desert in the world

The Atacama in what was not yet called Chile

11,000 years ago natives
cultivated vegetables
mined copper
buried women sitting up
dry mummies in the driest
                                        desert in the world

Way before the conquistadores came

Less than five hundred years have gone by
since they galloped through these green fields
Pedro de Valdivia came through

heading South looking for gold
dreaming of the ice of Antarctica
and the twelve cities of El Dorado
Yes he passed through here one night

He saw the stars I see

It would have taken him two years
to send a letter home to Spain
and get a reply
two years before he got a reply

I write to my son on a Spanish keyboard
where everything is askew
No letter no number no control button
where I expect it to be
laboring not to make mistakes

Wanting to know if the baby's all right
Is the baby all right

And then the lights go off

At precisely six o'clock each night
the lights go off
                    in San Pedro de Atacama.
Not to worry, says the owner
of the Internet Café
from the shadows comes his voice
                    Your computer
he says is on a battery
And in effect my screen keeps
                    glowing
in the semi-dark

barely enough to see the keys
So I keep at it
stumbling finger-blind in the dimness
with no eyes to guide me
to the right letter right word
Is the baby all right
Gobbledygook and mistakes
flash brightly on the screen and—
nonsense cryptic signs jabber babble
claptrap of light
Not to worry says the owner
as I try and try and try
The power will come back he says
soon soon they're just
switching to a bigger engine for the night

And then a few minutes later
a few mangled words later
the light blasts on again
a radio booms
shouts of joy shouts of relief
Maybe of anger   a pair of lovers
caught in the glare in the sudden plaza outside
caught against the adobe wall of the church outside
clinging to each other
under the Andes unprotected

Electricity surges everywhere

And my computer turns dark
screen blackened gone lost
lost this letter to my son
disappeared not even into cyberspace
simply swallowed

The battery couldn't take it
                    the owner says
At times it's this screen at times that screen
That's how it goes in San Pedro de Atacama
We'll give you your money back

But before I recompose the letter
How's the baby
How are you doing
Missing you
Don't whisper a word to him
                    about the computer
howling its silence
                    in the madness of the desert

Before

So this is how it happened

God Something Someone Some Force
was typing and things were going
Okay sort of
in the center of darkness
and then no lights and then fingers
and then mistakes and shadows
keys always where they're not supposed to be
God or Whatever half radiance wrote the Universe
And then with a bang
                    That was it
                    That's how it goes in San Pedro
We were all born
Something was born back then
Vainly trying 15 billion
                    years later

to make sense of the message

While in the Universe next door
the mailman delivered a letter on time
And everything was perfect
And there was no Hitler
And not one child
Not one not one
                                    died of cancer
Here I am here we are
stuck in this glory of ours
glitching a ride
trying to write letters
to our children and their children
before the lights go out
                                    yet again
yet again.

Ten Minutes

I sit here on the deck at the back of our house in Durham
here in North Carolina, far from home, far from Chile,
looking up at the big tree, the big pine tree that is dead
and needs to be cut down.
Yesterday the man said he would come by
                                today sometime
between 5 and 6 in the afternoon, he said
and I said yes, I'd be here, come on by,
and so I wait for the tree man, I wait watching
watching the forest that surrounds our house
for the tree man to come and cut down that dead tree.

The sun is going down, down the horizon behind me,
down the tree the brown light slides for ten minutes
minute by brown minute.

It has been here before this house was built before I was born.
Can it be as old as my father—ninety-four years old my father
my father who lives alone in Buenos Aires since my mother died.
I'll give him a call tonight.

Cars pass by unseen on the street nearby.
A solitary bird, silent, flies over my head.
Another bird, chattering, scolding, follows.
Only once does a breeze flow through
                                the so green leaves of other trees
taking its time before reaching me as I watch the tree that has died
but somehow still stands up so straight, so full of sky.
I can hear a plane overhead, and the sky is a pale chalk of blue
clear so clear and yet no plane, no plane. Only the sound.
And birds, birds suddenly. Not one lands on the tree, not one.

Do they know?

It is six o'clock, and the man has not come.
Nothing has happened. No one has knocked at the door.
Not even the phone has rung.

I will have to wait, I guess, for the man to come,
the man to come with his saw and look up at the tree
and tell me when he'll cut it down.
I guess I'll have to wait.

It's so quiet I can almost hear the world turn.
Almost.

I guess I'll have to wait.

Waving Good-Bye

For John Berger, written two weeks
before I heard of his death

Come to the mountains, you said,
but I never came, I never went to see you.
I stayed behind in the cities
at my twilight desk of dreams
among the bounty of my books
far too enthralled by awards and petitions
and the denizens of empty praise
to find the time to respond, John,
to that invitation with my body,
bring a strong back for the harvest,
come and see the men till and plow
the rough pig earth for the meager measure
of potatoes and wheat that will be stolen,
stolen by merchants and taxmen and time,
come before it is too late and there
is
    nothing
            left to see or reap or even grieve,
before these men and the women
who milked the cows dry and flicked the flies,
come before they disappear into the cities
where you will pass them on the street
and not know where they were born,
what they fled and bled or who or who
or who they loved in and out of death,
come, my friend, before it is too late,
too late for them and too late for you.

But I never came, John, I never went
to see you in the mountains.

Elegy for the Plants as They Are Harvested and Eaten

Gather us from the ground

Take me, take me, plunder us plunge into each plum sweetly
rape the sanctuary of the tree every little last grain the cypress is
in love with the smell of jasmine listen to the walnuts as they hit
and split the ground listen to the seed turn in the soil listen to the
stars in the song of the grass walnuts falling like echoing bones:
take me take me take me like the morning flower takes the rain
try us on like a garment we dance when we're broken open drink
me eat me slice me sup me cup me rub me dice and spice and rice
me into the wilderness of taste listen to the stars in the song of
the stones nothing goes to waste nothing goes to waste try me on
like a pomegranate lentils onions leeks split peas and don't forget
potatoes don't forget tomatoes take me for your vegetable pot no,
me, no, me, lemon juice from the lemon tree orange juice from
the wheel of chance come my beloved I am the radiant bride I'm
the bridegroom inside remember when you drank rain in the gar-
den that was for this that was for this like a candle in the sun
lights the way a bit more not true that it is useless that luminous
minimal mineral caress your cry in the throat is the secret cup
cinnamon cardamom ginger and sage chamomile fennel ginger
and garlic and salt simmer mix spice sprinkle black pepper and
cherries potatoes boil tomatoes from the summer of spinach and
lettuce take me take me take me a grotto of black pepper go to
the vineyard and milk the wind go to the milk plant and drink
the wine and sun take me rape me remember when you drank
rain in the garden remember me remember me remember me
your teeth and your throat are the secret cup come my beloved I
am the radiant bride I am the bridegroom inside into the wilder-
ness into the fruit's caress every last little grain remember when
you drank the garden in the rain remember when you grew in the
field near the sugarcane remember the taste remember nothing

nothing nothing ever goes to waste remember when you drank rain in the garden it was all for this it was all for this first and final kiss it was so we could heal

nothing ever dies

nothing ever really dies.

Shakespeare and Cervantes Write to Each Other on the Occasion of the Four Hundred Years of Their Simultaneous Disappearance from This World

"A Sonnet from Beyond Death by William Shakespeare for Miguel De Cervantes"

> Let me not to the marriage of true minds
> Admit impediment. Does it matter that you
> And I never met on the road that winds
> Between your Spain and the England that I knew?
>
> Ten years before we both died, forsaken,
> I was invited to your land and did not go.
> How I wish now that chance had been taken
> So your smiles could have relieved my woe.
>
> It would've been enough to pour out my soul
> Just once to someone able to understand
> And keep me company and make me whole.
> If we did not then face death and darkness hand
>
> In hand, at least this comfort exiles my regret:
> In the hearts of men, yes, we are forever met.

"A Sonnet from Beyond Death Whereby Miguel De Cervantes Responds to William Shakespeare"

> When to the sessions of sweet silent thought
> I summon up remembrance of things past,
> I too lament the many things we sought
> And could not possess. Though I never asked

To meet your grace nor heard your name declared
Now that I am hid in death's dateless night,
I understand what we could then have shared.
Your Prince of Denmark and my sad mad Knight

Were brothers as they lived and dreamt and died.
And here are we, in the vanished waste of time,
With eternity to play side by side,
Your Lear, my Squire, our loves, Prospero's rhyme.

So if I think on thee, dear soft friend,
All losses are restored and sorrows end.

A Question for Shakespeare and Cervantes

Who visited them as they lay dying in late April of 1616, those two men, one in Madrid, the other in Stratford-upon-Avon, who whispered a last word in their ears, a final question?

The story of our own death is the one experience we are unable to transmit to anybody else. If Cervantes and Shakespeare, despite their divine talent for words, cannot escape that iron rule of mortality, if we can never know exactly what went on in their minds as they perished, the temptation of eavesdropping on the last, concurrent moments of the two greatest literary giants of their age, and perhaps any age, is irresistible. It is a matter of using the very imagination with which they peopled and changed the world, the legacy of that imagination should help us listen to the voices that called on those writers on their deathbed.

So if it were up to us, who would we choose to approach Miguel de Cervantes in our stead as he dies, murmur something to William Shakespeare at the end of his life? Who might be invited to intervene? Forget the sobbing relatives, the avid clergy, the curious bystanders.

Someone else.

Someone to keep those authors gentle company as they breathed their last.

For Cervantes, there can be no doubt.

Don Quixote would be selected to ask that final question of his creator, pose it to the man who allowed him and his Squire to sally forth on the roads of La Mancha, seeking adventures in a land that no longer needed dreamers like them, a world that had no use for them save as entertainment. Perhaps Don Quixote, always so curious, would have first liked to grasp what so many of his future readers will ponder: how could a veteran soldier so buffeted by misfortune and misery ever come to write such a joyous work, fashion hope out of the ashes of illusions and sadness? Or perhaps that old man invented by Cervantes, tall and thin, insane and sagacious, would have extracted from his Maker some wisdom to guide his compatriots in the troubled times that plagued them, the same dilemmas our humanity faces centuries later.

But the Knight of the Sad Countenance fears squandering this one chance to address his Author about something absolutely crucial, something that has been worrying him since his inception. He knows this is his last quest. After so many frustrated fights for justice, so many failed enterprises, Don Quixote will not let himself get that final task wrong.

As to Shakespeare, his stage is inhabited by so many favorite characters that it is difficult to conjure up which of them would make an appearance on that day of reckoning. Wouldn't the Bard greet Falstaff and Rosalind, Juliet and Miranda and Puck with a smile, would he not understand that Lear and Macbeth, Othello and Malvolio might demand from him an explanation about their fate? Or would Shakespeare pluck Prospero from his island and thank him kindly for whatever music and magic might ease this farewell? But if Shakespeare gets to choose—and why would he not try and defeat loneliness as darkness descends?—one candidate stands out. The Prince of Denmark. Like Don Quixote, Hamlet—another performer of madness— might be tempted to plunge into the infinite enigmas his creator left behind. He could ask why Cordelia was not spared, why Ophelia had to drown, why Desdemona's love is so blind. Or query the mysteries of Shakespeare's existence, was he Catholic, where did he venture during those lost years, who inspired the Sonnets?

But the dusty hour of death is not for such matters.

Before the rest is silence, a question must be asked, room only for one essential word as the syllables of recorded time elapse.

The same word Don Quixote has readied for Cervantes.

What is it to be?

If we had only one word, one question to ask these two wonders of our species four hundred years after their noble hearts cracked and ceased to beat, what would it be?

One word that Hamlet would ask, that Don Quixote would ask, the one word that all children seek an answer to as soon as they can express themselves, the one question that each fellow human never tires of asking. The one question to which there is no definitive response, the response these two men, Shakespeare and Cervantes, pursued in everything they shaped and may have come closest to resolving, tentatively, grievously, miraculously.

That one word they hear as they say goodbye.

That one word.

Why?

THREE

A GRAIN OF WHEAT IN THE SILENCE

"Como un grano de trigo en el silencio,
pero a quién pedir piedad por un grano de trigo?"

(Like a grain of wheat in the silence,
but who to ask mercy for a grain of wheat?)

Pablo Neruda, *Residencia en la Tierra*

Reprieve

I awake again.

The card on which my name and my dates are written, date of birth, date of detention, the presumed date of death, that frail card has been handed to someone entering the Museum, that is all I know, that is supposed to be enough. Such are the rules of this universe, I am kept in the dark as to whether it is a man or a woman who reads the information, it might even be a child, of course, of course, who came to this place to learn about Memory, reflect upon the victims of that catastrophe, so the past will not be repeated. As if the past is not repeated endlessly for some, as if that could ever be avoided.

This is not the first time someone reads me back into this transitory existence, not the first time I live for the shudder of time it takes for whatever visitors are clasping my name in their hands to meander through the Museum and then, at the end, erase me, return these thoughts of mine to the anonymity of the box at the building's exit where my card, each time more threadbare, will repose until it is once more retrieved, if indeed I am once more retrieved and not shuffled away with other cards that are scruffy and frayed, incinerated to make room for somebody else plucked out of the fog of history.

So I must savor the brief spasm of this restitution while I can, while he or she who grasps the card and glances at my name and pronounces, generally with some difficulty, the foreign-sounding syllables of the place where I was murdered, I should be grateful for this circumstance, aware of how many are not afforded even these minutes of resurrection on somebody's imperfect, hesitant lips, I have not forgotten all the nameless denizens of the dark seething and sighing in the abyss where I came from, millions of them lost in the night of an interminable archive, never called, as

I have been over and over, to remember who I once was, the remains of who I am.

Not an easy journey.

The first time I was roused, as soon as I was extracted from the depths of a dreamless sleep meant to be eternal, the first time my name was read by some stranger in this cavernous Museum what immediately bit into me like a wild dog was the scene of my ending, those final pleading, cursing, desperate seconds just before those men—those men, their eyes and hands, that's what surfaced. Only natural, I would tell myself later, that the ultimate violence I had endured should flood my mind upon being unexpectedly jolted into wakefulness, no room to even wonder how such a miracle had been made possible.

That question was posed and resolved during my second awakening. I managed to eavesdrop, whether due to luck or design I still cannot fathom, on a conversation between the curator of this initiative and the director of the Museum as they congratulated themselves on how successful it had been. That's when I understood that I was part of a Memory Experiment, my name had been stumbled upon by some obscure scholar and reaped, along with a small number of others, from a cesspool of oblivion, each one of us and our three naked dates then inscribed on a card to be assigned, at random, to each visitor as a way of experiencing, however fleetingly, what the loss of one fellow human entails. That was the plan: pin a face on the tragedy, avoid overwhelming guests, as the director called them, with statistics that cannot embody the pain of each life snuffed out like a candle never to be relit.

Never to be relit? the curator asked. Never? Not true, she said, her words echoing like footsteps approaching and then receding in my mind, we'll prove it's not true. We can relight the candle, allow a flame to flicker and burn for the duration of each visit, at least that long and who knows if beyond. Did she have the slightest inkling, that guardian of my name and dates, that her plan would induce a dawn of discernment inside a select few of the

75

chosen dead, inside someone like me? Or is that also part of her project, that she has some hidden way of accessing the thoughts of those who are revived? No, no, that cannot be, she cannot be aware, she who is my Maker, that those nominated for this rescue operation lurk in the depths of infinity waiting to be recalled, that each card would turn into a portal, a hole in space and time through which we ebb and flow, and that once we have been granted this tattered respite, we are trapped here, we cannot refuse the memories that engulf us. How could she possibly guess what I am being forced to witness as my card is fingered and worn out?

Initially, it is true, only the final gasp of life, the terror of dying all over again, but then, on subsequent recurrences, I managed to stifle my surprise and revulsion, and gradually took control of my emotions, told myself that this was a chance to go beyond the murder into which I had thought I would be forever frozen, that had been my last thought as I died, this is it, there is no more, forever frozen, the very last words plummeting through my brain as my heart stopped. Yet here I am, there is no time to lose, I should repossess whatever less lethal segments I could from the only past bestowed upon me. My mother's smile when I tasted the cakes she had baked to celebrate my first day at school, that solitary secret kiss under a tree that must have been a willow because there was a brook nearby promising other kisses, other bodies pressing together on some morrow that never came, and venturing back to infancy, my inaugural memory, I slip a foot into a sea that is vast and auspicious and do not falter or fall because a hand is holding mine, I look up and it is my sister's and she nods her head reassuringly, she does not know then and does not know now that she will have no card, has not been blessed with even a few minutes of relief from the darkness, like my other sister has no card, like my two brothers and my father and my mother as I watched what was done to them and—so it is, so it is, I am cast back, no matter to what joyful memory I escape, my final moments, so similar to theirs, will always ambush me, catch up with me, drown everything else out like the wave's savage resolution when it knocked me into the sea that morning and my sister picked me up laughing, telling me that the ocean is salty because it has so many tears and we must not add to them.

I should have died that day, I should have let myself die that day, I would have if I had known what the future held, my sister would have drowned herself, we'd have sunk into the deep together, embraced like seaweed, if she and I, if we——. But no, this is my miracle and I must not scorn it, I am the only one of the family, the youngest of us all, chosen for this experiment, there are not enough researchers to uncover all the names, not enough visitors in this city, in this country, in this world, to read that many cards, I am the one who is drawn from the well, it is my destiny to awaken and remember and then be recycled to start this process all over again.

If I get another chance, that is.

If this does not happen to be the last time that I will rise from the ashes, that is the closing thought simmering into me now as the visit ends—can it have been so ephemeral, why did whoever was my host not spend more hours at the Museum, why did he, or she, or she, somebody's mother, not tarry and utter once more like an incantation the dates and my name and the even more unpronounceable name of the place where I died, why do my hosts always wander through the exhibits clutching the card nervously, not knowing how where what to really do with it when all should be so clear. Why do they not settle into a quiet corner and sit down as one would on a bench in a cemetery bereft of flowers and prayers, why do they not try to speak to me, ask me questions as they look slowly one more time at the increasingly shriveled card that is my gateway to this voice that barely knows how to whisper to itself the fear that this may be the last time, why do they not realize what secrets still need to be disinterred from my vanishing presence, for their good and mine, my future and theirs, are they not also destined to disappear someday, why

77

do they now approach the exit where the box looms ahead into which they have been instructed to drop my increasingly emaciated card, why do my visitors always obey those instructions so blindly and are so eager to leave, so anxious to breathe in the fresh air of the street outside and return to their hot meals and entertainment, why did those strangers not take me home with them, take home with them the memories of the sister who could not protect me despite her love, I can feel myself fading, why did they not, at least one of them, why did somebody not, back then before I was executed, back then and now as I say good-bye to the only self I ever inhabited, why am I fading as my card falls forever frozen into the pit of this box, why do they, why are you about to forget me?

For Sarajevo, After a Thousand and One Days and Nights of Siege

If this were a fairy-tale
    If this were the night
                        after
    the thousand and one nights
If this were the next night
                        after
    the thousand and one nights
If this were a fairy-tale
    and Scherezade had just finished
    telling her final story
    and the man who can order her death
    had relented
If this were a fairy-tale where
    Scherezade would not have to invent
                     one more story
                     one more story

    so the night could end
                in one more dawn
        for her
                and those other women
    waiting for their death
                unto rubble.

If this were a fairy-tale, Sarajevo,
    and we were Scherezade
    here outside in this world
    sending you prayers

Written for a Sarajevo-UNICEF benefit at New York's Union Theatre on January 29th, 1995, the 1,000st day of the siege.

—as we have—
for a thousand and one nights
so the dawn would come
there in Sarajevo
If this were a fairy-tale
and you had sent us
—as you have—

over and over
your Sarajevo stories of one more cracked dawn
your Sarajevo whispers of one more shared
naked night of scars
breaking the siege with stories
If this were a fairy-tale
you in Sarajevo
we in New York
you in Sarajevo
we in Santiago
Scherezade in Sarajevo
Scherezade in New York
calling to each other
for a thousand and one dawns,
keeping each other alive
If this were a fairy-tale,
then this would be the day
this is it—the day, the day,
the night, the dawn,
this is when you should awaken there
in Sarajevo
under that sky
we see only on our screens
If this were a fairy-tale
right now you would awaken
right now I say
you have to be awakening

to the sounds of peace
and children in the street
        playing like children
who awaken without fear
        right now I say
If this were a fairy-tale
        where many brides awaken
        and many brothers await
If this were a fairy-tale
        a thousand and one nights of betrayal
        a thousand and one nights of siege
awaiting death
        would have been should have been enough.
Yes. Let me say it again.
Should have been enough.
How can it be
in this world
        that a thousand and one nights
are not
are not
        can never be
                        enough.

I think of Scherezade now
                        as she awakens
        on the dawn after
        her thousand and one nights.
I watch her watch the dawn.
I watch her listen to life purse her lips open her mouth
        prepare herself
                        for one more day
        that could be her last.
She already knows the story
even if in this world

a thousand and one stories
are not
are not
    can never be

                enough
she already knows the story
she will tell us
        again
            and again
        and again
tonight
      and tomorrow
           and again tonight.

Farewell and Dawn

for the families of Francisco Gomes de Medeiros,
Alfredo Villatoro and Regina Martínez, three of so
many murdered journalists in Latin America

Though it be the last word I write, my love,
though it be the last, the last, the last of them all,
though it be my last word, my love,
                    your last word,
the last word of mine you read, my love,
the last breath heard
that I live and breathe,
I will not cease, my love,
we will not allow
                    unsaintly death
to increase its malignant undertow.

This is my house, your sainted land,
our line of last and sweet defense,
my word as the closing quiet blow
against war's outraging violence,
though it be the last I write, my love,
the last, the last, the last word
I breathe, however small,
however distant what you read,
whispering against death, unsaintly and insane,
only truth, this truth so marginal,
my defiant and final defense
of our earth as it turns,
this word,

This poem was part of a campaign by Pen International.

though it be the last
though it be the last word,
though it be the last word I ever write, my love,
my bread, my body, my family, my land,
though it be my last birth,
though it be the last, my love,
though it be
though it be
though it be
the last window
of our house as it burns.

Poem for the Grandchildren of Three Five O_2

Oh dear Oh dear Oh dear
What should I do?
The polar bears are dying out.
Oh dear Oh dear
The children cannot breathe.
What should I do?
The elephants have nowhere
                 to flee.
The elephants Oh dear it's true.
What should I
          can I
                must I do?

Oh dear Oh
Three Five O
Oh dear that scares me scares me so
Oh dear we won't survive
Three Five O up in the sky
and no more birth
and it's good-bye.

The seventh extinction is on its way.
Can the eighth extinction be far behind?

Oh dear
It's much too big for little me

Not a tree not a tree
not even a shade of green.

Written in 2009 at the request of Bill McKibben and Rebecca Solnit as part of a campaign in support of 350.org.

Oh dear oh dear
The cities all
                    vanished
                              wiped out.
The drought the plague the black dark
                                        death.
            Not even a bird
                    for our last breath.
And there's nothing
                        nothing
                                    nothing
I can do.

Much too big for you for him for her for me.
We're melting the sea.

Oh dear

Oh.

Oh if I could only trust
the hand that is close
the hand that is here

Oh if I could count all over again
but not with dread.

Maybe one plus one makes more than two
maybe three can be three million strong
in fact
maybe five means five billion tall
ready to act

to make that O the sign of birth
and not the mark
                    of nightmares long
                    and lonely bread.

Three Five O
Dot.Org
Three Five O

organizers bold
bells that toll
climbers on the mountain
divers under the reef

we'll come together

we'll come together
in every corner of the earth

we have very little time
but we have each other

we have very little time
but I have little you
and you have little me

and time enough for us
to act and be free
        as long as we have each other
one hand in my hand
there can only be birth

my dear oh my dear

there's just love enough and time
now and here

now and here

to act and then nothing
                            nothing
                                    nothing
to fear.

Anything Else Would Have Tasted like Ashes

for Desmond Tutu, in memoriam and in my memory

1

I don't want to pretend I was a hero
In the beginning
 I had neither pen nor paper to work with

2

But you don't live your life in fear
And give people power over you
Who can
 create fear
It would be better to die early

Anything else would have tasted like ashes

That's what you know

3

Few and far between
Few and far between
Something is there
A light is there
I did what I had to do
Knowing this knowing this
The poor of the world are crying out

This poem was created using the literal words, phrases and sayings of human
rights activists from around the world as gathered by Kerry Kennedy in her
book, *Speak Truth to Power* (Umbrage), the basis for a play I wrote *Speak
Truth to Power: Voices from Beyond the Dark,* which, since its premiere at the
Kennedy Center in the year 2000, has been performed hundreds of times
around the world, both by concerned citizens, students and some of our great-
est actors and actresses.

4

That's what you know
Anything else would have tasted like ashes
That's what you know
The poor of the world are crying out
The poor of the world are crying out
For schools and doctors, not generals and guns

You just have to believe in what you're doing, that's all

5

I was never alone
That's what you know
Only another person can give me hope

                                        because

Only another person can take hope

                                        away from me

We did what we had to do, that's all

Anything else would have tasted like ashes

6

Did it take courage?
It took stubbornness   Stubbornness   Like a metal chord inside
The feeling of inner strength like a metal chord inside
So our past does not become your children's future

Anything else would have tasted like ashes

Knowing this knowing this
We owe something to the people left behind

7

And God dusts us off and God says, "Try again."
God says, "Try again."
God says,
Life will only belong to you once
only this once
And so, we continue
knowing this knowing this
If we bring people to their own best hearts
they will respond

That's what you know
we were never alone

8

And so, we continue
knowing this knowing this
that this moment might well be

                                        our last

waiting, waiting,
waiting in the dark for the truth

We were never really alone

9

I don't want to pretend I was a hero
I did what I had to do, that's all
It's really so simple
Anything else, anything else would have tasted like ashes
That is what you know

The work has just begun

10

That is what we know
We did what we had to do
The work has just begun.

Last Will and Testament

When they tell you I'm not a prisoner,
don't believe them.
They'll have to admit it
someday.
When they tell you they released me,
don't believe them.
They'll have to admit
it's a lie
someday.
When they tell you I'm in France
don't believe them.
Don't believe them when they show you
my false I.D.
don't believe them.
Don't believe them when they show you
the photo of my body, don't believe them.
Don't believe them when they tell you
the moon is the moon,
if they tell you the moon is the moon,
if they tell you that this is my voice on tape,
that this is my signature on a confession,
if they say a tree is a tree
don't believe them,
don't believe
anything they tell you
anything they swear to
anything they show you,
don't believe them.
And finally
when
that day

comes
when they ask you
to identify the body
and you see me
and a voice says
we killed him
the poor bastard died
he's dead
when they tell you
that I am
completely absolutely definitely dead
don't believe them,
don't believe them, don't believe them.
     no les creas
     no les creas
     no les creas.

A Sort of Epilogue with Help from Francisco de Quevedo

Some years ago, I was among one hundred men to be asked by Amnesty International to select a poem that made me cry. The poem that I chose was written by Francisco de Quevedo back in the seventeenth century. The reader of this book will have already encountered the final lines of that very poem as an epigraph to the middle section of this work. I now reproduce that sonnet by Quevedo—both in Spanish and English—as a fitting way to end this volume, followed by my own reasons on why it moves me to tears.

Though that meditation evokes how the love I feel for my Angélica might persist beyond death, I can only hope that my mother and father, to whom this book is also dedicated, might have subscribed to those words before they died, perhaps they are whispering them to us at this very moment.

I can only hope that both Quevedo's sonnet and my response to it may allow readers to commune with the deeper vision that sustains all the other poems from beyond death that dwell in this book.

"Amor Constante Más Allá De La Muerte"
Francisco de Quevedo (1580-1645)

Cerrar podrá mis ojos la postrera
Sombra que me llevare el blanco día,
Y podrá desatar esta alma mía
Hora, a su afán ansioso lisonjera;

Mas, no de esotra parte, en la ribera,
Dejará la memoria, en donde ardía:
Nadar sabe mi llama el agua fría,
Y perder el respeto a ley severa.

Alma, a quien todo un dios prisión ha sido,
Venas, que humor a tanto fuego han dado,
Médulas, que han gloriosamente ardido:

Su cuerpo dejará, no su cuidado;
Serán ceniza, mas tendrá sentido;
Polvo serán, mas polvo enamorado.

"Love Constant Beyond Death"
(Translated by Margaret Jull Costa)

Though my eyes be closed by the final
Shadow that sweeps me off on the blank white day
And thus, my soul be rendered up
By fawning time to hastening death.

Yet memory will not abandon love
On the shore where first it burned:
My flame can swim through coldest water
And will not bend to laws severe.

Soul that was prison to a god,
Veins that fueled such fire,
Marrow that gloriously burned—

The body they will leave, though not its cares;
Ash they will be, but filled with meaning;
Dust they will be, but dust in love.

My Final Words

It is the last line that does it, the tears come from beyond me
and perhaps from beyond death. The eyes that shed those tears

will become dust, the eyes that have seen over and over the love of my life, Angélica, the woman who helped me survive exile and tribulations and peopled my world with hope, those eyes will have been closed by the final shadow. And yet, the *polvo*, the dust, is *enamorado*, is in love. Except that there are no words in English that can offer us the equivalent of *enamorado* or *enamoramiento*, so much so that I have had a correspondence with my friend, the extraordinary Spanish author Javier Marías, about the right translation into English for his equally extraordinary novel, entitled *Los Enamoramientos*, and we reached the conclusion that there was no perfect fit for such a word, not in English, not in any language.

Quevedo knew this many centuries ago and finished his poem with that word, which tells us that we are filled with love, we fall into love as if into an abyss, we ascend to its invitation to "enamorar," a verb that enhances what both lovers must do, make someone love me, find myself overflowing with love. That last verse never fails to make me cry. The laws of the universe discovered by physics assure humanity that we are composed of atoms and that protons and neutrons and electrons will scatter and rejoin, that everything is connected, that when we drink a glass of water or shed a tear, some slight marrow of Shakespeare or Brecht or Rumi, are submerged in the depths of the liquid coupling of hydrogen and oxygen, the cosmos as a giant blender, making our every cell ultimately immortal. I am not religious and do not believe, as Quevedo did, that the soul will subsist, that God will greet us once our body has finished its course of skin and bone and flesh. But this I do believe: my wife and I have sworn to mix our ashes, to be dust together for eternity. *Polvo seremos, mas polvo enamorado.* Angélica and I will be dust but dust in love. How can I not cry with joy, for myself, for her, for all of us on this earth that will itself turn to dust, ashes to ashes, yes, but ashes in love?

And now, my final words in this book.

Requiem for Some *Cenizas*

He had told her his ashes would be in love with her, that's how enduring and eternal his devotion was, but never expected it to be true.

Words, she had answered, laughing but also a bit sad, you're so good at words, if only words could make miracles happen, if only death did not conquer all. Let's content ourselves, that is what she had said, with every moment of love to be squeezed out of the here and now, come here, she had said, come now, she said, forget the ashes you promise, your *cenizas enamoradas*, forget the forever that is beyond the grave that you promise and kiss these lips of mine, you silly man, *mi amor*, suck everything you can suck from my body because that is all there is. Our flesh is already saying good-bye, we grow older with each second that passes, and we must make haste, or we will be gone, like your words are already gone, vanished like ashes in the wind.

Despite her objections and the sweetness that would always follow, he had persisted from time to time with his vow that he would be waiting for her if he died first or seek her out beyond the shore of death if she was to leave before he did. All through their lives he had resurrected those words whenever the occasion allowed them, they had ended up being like a prop that he recurred to like a cane an old man uses to cross the road on his last stumbling legs. And she had ceased to mock him, tolerated their repetition as long as they were not too frequently announced. In effect, she realized that he needed to express that pledge and half-believe it as a consolation against the certainty that they both were bound to die someday and without each other, starless in the permanent night of extinction.

She had even smiled at him through the glass partition that sealed her off from the world and from him, she had managed a smile in that isolation ward because she could not squeeze his hand or invite him to suck every cell in her body, to fill herself with him, the here was dying and the now as well, separated because that was the only way for the virus that rampaged inside her not to contaminate him, the man who had visited what was inside her over so many decades and yet had never entirely known what was going on, like now, inside her head.

And that had been the last time he had said that he would be ashes in love, the last time they played that game with words that came and went, a rite of passage rather than a conviction, that moment when she had smiled at his poetic silliness, turned out to be the last time he had spoken of *cenizas enamoradas* to her because when he returned the next morning, her eyes were closed and only a ventilator kept her breathing, barely up and down, that chest upon which his head had rested so its beat could slip into his beat, barely seeing anything through the glass partition.

No smiles possible on those lips anymore.

Through the next days and nights of vigil, she could not respond to that vow, and he had therefore lapsed into silence, unable to understand that her lack of an outward reaction did not mean she could not hear what he might say.

And then she was gone, just like that, no longer now, never again here. She was gone and he refused to comfort himself with that promise of an infinity of love beyond death, it was a lie that could not compensate for her absence, the empty house and the empty bed and the empty kitchen, that black hole in his empty life. She had been right, words do not create miracles, and they could not bring her back, his fingers would never touch and tangle hers, that glass partition had been a prelude and a forecast of what awaited them, a preparation of what was already coming for her and would come for him and, eventually, for every mortal under the sun.

And he told himself that no, not even when he scattered her ashes in their favorite forest, not even then, as some were to settle on the ground and some to dust the leaves and some wrap around the trees and some carried away by a breeze that would recall how she ruffled his hair, not even then could he dare to hope that those ashes might be waiting for him, not even then would he want to pronounce those words that she could not hear. He had said them to her by her bedside, on the other side of that glass partition, and despite the undeniable fact that she had smiled he could now not doubt that, as she had predicted, they were no more than words when confronted by the impossibility of reaching across that inconsolable divide.

So it was with relief and astonishment that he understood, a few months later, as his own body burnt in the crematorium, it was with gratitude that each small bird of a cell in his body awoke to the truth of what he had foretold, that he was assuredly dead but that the ashes were alive with her memory, he was still falling into her, part of cosmic dust, he would still be visiting her after the sun exploded and the universe went dark and cold, nothing is ever lost, there was not even a need for his ashes to meet her in the forest where both wife and husband were scattered, he heard his body singing as the flames consumed it, if you die not with love you have not lived, if you do not die of love you have not lived, forever and ever and ever after, amen.

That is what I imagine he is thinking, my husband, as he watches me dying in this hospital, my eyes closed but my ebbing mind still alive enough to hope that this is what *mi amor* believes will happen to me, to him, to both of us.

I will soon—we will all soon—find out.

Some Words of Thanks and *Gracias*
from This Side of Death

Thanks is not enough acknowledgment for those who kept me alive so I could write the words in this book.

For that, I need the Spanish into which I was born and where I still reside.

For that, I need *gracias.*

Because *gracias* also contains cognates and resonances in English and echoes of the Spanish and of all those men and women, long gone, who forged the word into meaning through the centuries so I could use it now.

Gracias recalls grace, what some say or pray before a meal as thanks for what they are about to receive. And gracias suggests inside itself the gratification and *agrado* I get from those who love and sustain me as I labor with what I hope is *gracia*, flair, ease of movement, a certain elegance and flow. *Gracias* resounds, above all, with *la gracia*, which, as in the English grace, invokes the quality of mercy, what is given gratuitously, without a second thought, without hoping for some sort of reward but simply out of the mystery of caring for another.

Due to all this, when I say *gracias* to those I will now name, I am full of gratefulness, a word that means so much more than a mere thanks. They have kept me from *desgracia*, from misfortune. They have taught to never be *ingrato*, ungrateful, unpleasant. They have even been nice enough to find me *gracioso*, funny, from time to time.

So, *gracias* to Angélica, Rodrigo, Joaquín, Isabella, Catalina, Deena, Heather, Cece, Nathalie, Ryan, Ana María, Pedro, Pato, Marisa, and *grazie* to Al, Mary, Greg, Kathy, John, Pela, Gary, Kayleigh, Emmy, Kirby, Sharon, and *merci* to Queno, Antonio, Nora, Elizabeth, Soledad, Guillermo, and *obrigado* to Mark, Susan, Joe, Colum, Bill, José Miguel, Gina, Bruce, Miriam,

Antonia, and *danke* to Max, Maartje, Jacqueline, Bert, Hedda, and *gracias infinitas* to all my dead, Fanny and Adolfo, Julio and Harold and Desmond and, of course, our dear Eric, all those who still speak to me from the other side.

And the word thanks is also not enough for those who helped, very concretely, to bring this book to life.

So, *gracias* to my agents, Jacqueline Ko, Kristi Murray, Jennifer Bernstein, and to my assistant, Suzan Senerchia and the librarians at Duke. And *gracias* to Susan Brenneman who welcomed my words from the other side of death in the op ed pages of the *Los Angeles Times* and Wendy Lesser, who gave Cervantes and Shakespeare a place to meet in *The Threepenny Review*, and above all, *muchas gracias,* to the remarkable Tom Englehardt who, in *Tomdispatch*, created many spaces so these words from beyond the beyond could reach mortal ears. And to Nicky Parker at Amnesty and Jemimah Steinfeld at Index on Censorship, and to my editors at Open Democracy and at *Guernica* and the journal *Eleven Eleven, gracias también.*

Finally, *gracias* a Nicolás Kanellos, my editor y amigo, who believed in this book and turned that belief into work and advice and sustenance, and others at Arte Público Press, (Gabriela Baeza Ventura, Adelaida Mendoza and Marina Tristán), who labored so these voices could find pages on which to be printed and deployed and attended to.

When a new book is published, the author receives congratulations. Congratulate, related to grace and *gracias.* But if congratulations are in order, if readers should feel it is worth the prayer, they should direct their gratitude to the gracious and graceful people I have listed here. Without them, *este libro no existiría,* this book would not have been born, would not have had a chance to speak from the other side of death.

To all of you, congratulations, another word that resounds with the glow of *gracias.*

Poems previously published include:

"A Question for Shakespeare and Cervantes," *The Threepenny Review*, Fall, 2016.

"Amor constante más allá de la muerte," *Poems that Make Grown Men Cry: 100 Men on Words that Move Them*, Simon and Schuster, New York, London, 2014.

"Christopher Columbus Has Words from the Other Side of Death for Captain John Whyte, Who Rebaptized Saddam International Airport as His Troops Rolled into It," *openDemocracy*, February 25, 2003.

"Dante Alighieri Has Words from the Other Side of Death for Donald J. Trump as His Presidency Ends," *TomDispatch*, October 22, 2020.

"For Sarajevo, After a Thousand and One Nights of Siege," *Los Angeles Times*, February 13, 1995.

"Glitch," *Eleven Eleven*, California College of Arts, issue 9, 2010.

"Hammurabi, the Exalted Prince Who Made Great the Name of Babylon, Has Words from the Other Side of Death for Donald Rumsfeld," *TomDispatch*, September 5, 2003.

"James Buchanan, the 15th President of the United States Has Words of Encouragement from the Other Side of Death for Donald J. Trump Just Before His Inauguration in January 2017," *Los Angeles Times*, January 19, 2017.

"Long Forgotten," *Guernica*, April 15, 2015.

"Pablo Picasso Has Words for Colin Powell from the Other Side of Death," *TomDispatch*, February 03, 2003. The poem was subsequently made into a cantata, "Voices from Guernica," by composer Klaus Huber.

"Poem for the Grandchildren of Three Five O$_2$," 350.org website on July 22, 2009.

"Salvador Allende Has Words for Barack Obama from the Other Side of Death," *TomDispatch*, October 9, 2011.

"William Blake Has Words from the Other Side of Death for Laura Bush, Lover of Literature," *San Francisco Chronicle*, July 25, 2004.